RV & Campi͟ ͟ ͟ ͟ ͟ ͟ ͟ ͟ ͟

Healthy Living on a Budget

The Ultimate Guide for Recipes, Tips, and Tricks, for the Road Nomad Lifestyle

Enjoy Poultry, Seafood, Vegetarian & Vegan Full Meal Recipes – Desserts Included)

By

Lynn Roberts

Thames & Tower
HOUSE SERIES

Cover Designer & Art Director

Rebecca Floyd

1st Edition

Contents

Introduction

So you're cruising down the highway in your trusty RV, bopping your head to your favorite tunes and having the time of your carefree life.

It doesn't take long before something feels amiss—your mind starts to wander, your emotions get jumbled, and there's this uncomfortable, nagging sensation in your gut.

Before you know it, you're irritable, grumpy, and what was once a beautifully magnificent stretch of road ahead now becomes an intolerable test of your patience. You think to yourself that this is it, the ultimate challenge on the road—hunger.

When hunger strikes, there's not much you can do other than to grab a bite to eat immediately before you unleash your tummy tantrums on your innocent companions.

But do you stop at a fast-food joint and just grab the first thing that you see? Do you indulge in those greasy, icky, unhealthy, sinful snacks and just eat now and regret it later?

Just because you're living in an RV doesn't mean you should sacrifice your health! There are plenty of wholesome habits you can adapt to your mobile lifestyle to ensure that you stay fit and fab even when you're on the road.

Aside from regular exercise and the proper mindset, you can utilize these easy, healthy, budget, and RV-friendly recipes to keep your beneficial eating habits on track!

Healthy RV Living

When you're going on an RV trip, it's a must to pack some delightful little treats like chips, sweets, and snacks for on the road. After all, whether you're going on an extended trip or just out for a quick vacation, it's always a joy to indulge every now and then.

But while you're out there enjoying the great outdoors and the big, wide-open road, it's not a good idea to simply derive the entirety of your nourishment from junk food, is it?

You need to make room for actual, real, healthy meals if you don't want your health to suffer, especially if you will be engaging in energy-draining activities like hiking, canoeing, or cycling.

Thankfully, you don't have to spend a whole lot of money just to keep yourself fit. You can forego the extra sugars, unnecessary salts, and unwanted cholesterol simply by committing to a healthier lifestyle on the road—and that includes getting exercise as well as eating the right kind of food.

Don't ever believe in the myth that healthier meals are more expensive and take longer to prep! The easy, budget-friendly, and RV-friendly recipes in this book can change all that.

Chuck the common misconception of healthy meals being unsavory out the window.

But first, here are some quick tips on how you can live healthier in an RV even without involving your appetite:

Stick to a regular schedule.

When you're living carefree in an RV, it's easy to forget all about proper timelines and schedules because you know you can pretty much sleep in and wake up any time you want to.

While it's truly liberating to control your own time, it's still very unhealthy to wake up late and sleep late or to do so at irregular intervals.

Besides, spending all day in your pajamas can quickly spiral you into a depression and might even drain you of any energy you actually have.

Why not get up and about and exercise when you can?

You don't need a fully equipped gym to work up a sweat.

All you need to do is lace up your running shoes and head outside for some fresh air and a healthy dose of Vitamin-D.

Seemingly small and insignificant routines, like brewing a hot cup of coffee at eight in the morning, can help ground you and keep life's stability intact.

When you're always on the move, anything that keeps you grounded is a treasure in itself—something that is precious and must be well-kept every day.

Home-cooked is best.

Just because you are traveling in an RV doesn't mean you're vacationing full-time! (OK, maybe it does if you're retired...)

The RV way of life is not about eating too much, spending too much, and throwing caution to the wind all the while burning a hole in your wallet.

Your life in a motor home isn't just a quick getaway— it's a lifestyle. If you really want to keep fit and keep those blood sugar levels in check, then cooking from your RV is your best bet.

Air and water quality.

Speaking of cooking in your motor home, you have to make sure that your RV is properly equipped with good ventilation to keep from reducing the quality of your indoor air.

You can also use essential oils to help purify your indoor air if you want to.

As for your drinking water, it can be more challenging to ensure that your water is free from bacteria and viruses, especially since you're often traveling from locale to locale.

As such, you should make sure that you have a proper water filter system in place in your RV.

Maximize your RV living!

Being at one with the great outdoors gives you instant access to Vitamin D, fresh air, and the relaxing sights and sounds of nature.

When you stretch your legs and head outside, you get to meet new people along the way, and you discover new places at different campgrounds.

You are also able to broaden your horizons with new knowledge each time. The natural cycle of the sun rising and setting also gets your body in tune with its natural cycle, letting you wake up when the sun is up and helping you sleep better when evening comes.

The independence and feeling of freedom lifts your mood and reduces stress levels, allowing for a healthier, happier life.

Living in an RV definitely has its healthy perks built-in! All you need to do is to maximize your experience to achieve your ultimate wellness on the road.

RV Exercise Regimen

When you're cruising in your motor home, you might have a tendency to stay inside and sit down all day while you're on the road.

The danger here is that people who sit down for more than 23 hours every week are at a greater risk of having a heart attack.

Plus, sitting down all the time can cause lower back pain, which is definitely not a good thing!

The key here is to squeeze in some time—and space!—to exercise, even while you're inside your RV. Think it's impossible? Nothing is impossible if you set your mind to it!

Even when you're stuck inside a small space, you can still engage in plenty of exercises and feel the burn.

For instance, even simple lunges can be considered exercise and can keep the unwanted calories at bay—it certainly beats sitting down and staying still all day.

Aside from lunges, some front squats, wall sits, and workouts with resistance bands can help you move without requiring a great deal of space.

Resistance bands and stability balls can be easily stored away. They can be deflated when not in use and then re-inflated with a pump so that they don't get in the way of the limited space you have in your motor home.

When you're out and about at campsites, bike, hike, and explore to your heart's content - as long as you keep moving!

Don't shy away from TV workouts.

You might think that TV workouts are cheesy, but they'll be your best friend when you have limited space and are stuck indoors.

You can invest in a few aerobic exercise videos, or even subscribe to a few YouTube channels, to get your heart pumping.

Yoga sessions are also easy to do when you have limited space—plus, there are plenty of yoga poses and routines that can help soothe aching muscles and tired joints from driving all day.

Invest in a mini, indoor gym.

An assortment of gym equipment now has more compact and more portable counterparts so that you can live the free RV life without sacrificing your cardiovascular fitness.

You can invest in a foldable exercise bike or a foldable walking pad that you can set out and fold up as needed.

These tools can help you put in a little extra sweat on more lethargic days so that you can get the endorphins up and running and recharged for another full day ahead.

Simple workouts work wonders.

With just an ordinary chair as your "exercise tool," you can perform knee extensions while sitting down. You can also do a backstretch by folding forward and touching your head to your knees from a seated position.

For a wall push-up, stand back from a wall or even your refrigerator with your arms at shoulder height. Place your hands firmly on the flat surface in front of you and lean forward.

Tighten your abs as you lean forward with your whole body, and make sure to come upon the balls of your feet.

You can also do planks on the floor or even half planks if the workout is too much for you. Remember, the longer you hold your position, the better the workout will be.

There really are limitless ways you can get the blood flowing and the heart pumping even while you're cruising in an RV!

All you have to do is to be creative and to really commit yourself to the workout. Those muscles aren't going to tone themselves!

RV Kitchen Management

When you have a properly stocked kitchen, chances are, you're not going to be splurging on unhealthy junk food.

Operating a fully equipped kitchen in such a small space and with limited resources can be a challenge.

The best thing to do is to choose your tools wisely and to pick the ones that you can maximize the most.

You need to make your kitchen as appealing as possible so that you will be more encouraged to whip up a nice meal. Creating an appealing kitchen means having the right kind of tools and equipment in it.

Now, this is not to say that you should stock up on everything just so you can have a fully equipped space that's decked to the nines with no more space for the actual food.

You still need to have enough storage room to keep the ingredients that you are going to be cooking with!

When you hit the road in a tight space, you might be too stressed out about not having enough room to move around when you're prepping meals.

You need to keep shopping to a minimum because you're going for budget-friendly meals.

Stocking the Galley

Here are your kitchen must-haves that will bring magic to your meals in a pinch:

Condiments are king.

Unsurprisingly, seasonings add flavor and spice to an otherwise dull meal. You should never run out of spices in a kitchen, even if you're cruising down the long, open road.

Condiments add variety to your food and can ensure flavors are versatile.

Basic condiments include:

- Salt

- Sugar

- Pepper

- Ketchup

- Honey

- Dried herbs

For instance, if you have some canned beans on hand, you can turn them into chili, whip them up into a healthy salad, serve them as a side dish, or mash them up into a tasty dip!

It's always a good idea to have spices on hand for when you need to switch it up every now and then instead of sticking to one kind of flavor for every meal.

Make room for multi-purpose.

Because you have such limited space in your RV, make sure that your tools are as multi-purpose as possible.

Having supplies that can double as something else will save you tons of storage space for the things that matter the most.

Pot lids can work double-time to cover skillets and saucepans, and colanders can drain your pasta as well as double as a serving bowl for healthy greens.

Wide plates can also serve as lids, but just remember to be careful when handling all the heat. In the kitchen, it's always about safety first!

Save up for staples.

Your pantry should be fully stocked with the essentials to avoid rummaging through your goods at the last minute only to find that you lack the basics.

Plus, last-minute grocery shopping almost always ends in unnecessary spending!

To stay within budget all the time, you should never run out of the following:

- Coffee

- Tea

- Mustard

- Mayonnaise

- Ketchup

- Hot sauce

- Relish

- Worcestershire sauce

- Salt

- Pepper

- Sugar or sweeteners of choice

- Honey

- Oregano

- Chili powder

- Basil

- Garlic powder

- Cumin

- Bouillon cubes

- Cereal

- Olive oil

- Rice

- Beans

- Canned meat like tuna, chicken, and shrimp

- Canned veggies like corn, artichokes, and green beans

Invest in good equipment.

Aside from the basic pots and pans, lids, plates, and utensils, your kitchen should have this essential equipment:

- Kitchen knife

- Cheese grater

- Tongs

- Blender (can be a hand/stick blender)

- Measuring cups and spoons

- Slow cooker/Crockpot

Your stove or oven should be sized reasonably enough to feed the people in your household. You can even have a few muffin cups on hand if you ever feel like baking. Muffin cups can also be used to portion out small size snacks, peanut butter, or other condiments.

Be efficient when it comes to maximizing your space, and always take note of your perishables.

You wouldn't want to lunch on expired munchies and have a funky odor in your RV to boot.

Plus, you should also try and save some space to stock leftovers—just make sure that you do finish them the next day so as not to keep them sitting there forever. Efficiency and not wasting food is key!

Crockpots are also invaluable when traveling in an RV, as well as instant pots or maybe even a collapsible colander.

Airtight storage is very important when you're stocking up your pantry, so invest in some rectangle and square containers that fit nicely in your cupboard to steer clear of all the clutter.

Make sure your plates and utensils are lightweight and easy to wash so that you won't have to spend extra money on disposable plates and forks. You'll even help out Mother Nature that way!

Also, you should have a roll-up drying rack that you can just tuck under the sink when you're done washing.

Maximize your kitchen space.

With all that stuff, you might think that it's impossible to fit everything into such a small and cramped space.

The thing is that if you look hard enough, you will discover small nooks and crannies that you can transform into efficient space-saving storage hacks in your RV.

Here are some ideas for maximizing the small space you have available in your RV kitchen:

- Hang organizers inside the doors with hooks with suction for lightweight items.

- Mini bag clips with magnets can hang on metal surfaces for lists, recipes, small pouches, dish towels, kitchen supplies, and plastic containers.

- Install a magnetic strip on your fridge for metal items.

- Cut Velcro strips to custom sizes and mount them to any flat surface, as RV's are movable, and so are your kitchen items!

Cost-effective and Healthy Recipes

Now that we've covered how important it is to live healthily and simply on the road let's get into the exciting recipes you should definitely try out in your motor home.

These recipes are not too extravagant—after all, we're aiming to cook healthily with cheap and affordable ingredients you can get from your local grocery store, or maybe something you already have in your pantry.

While you're traveling, you may also want to take advantage of farmer's markets, and local produce stands.

That's a great way to support the local farmers wherever you end up staying for a while, and also to cheaply acquire some super fresh produce.

Recipes with Red Meat

Meat, meat, meat! Oh, what would we do without meat?

As a good source of protein, meat has truly become a household staple in most homes today.

With these easy and affordable recipes, you don't have to break the bank to indulge in meaty goodness, especially while you're on the road!

Russian Cabbage Soup (Serves 4)

Here's a sweeter alternative to your average soup where the cabbage is the star of the show.

After all, nothing beats the warmth that a bowl of soup can bring, especially when you're out and about and hightailing it on the highway.

There's just something all-too-comforting about soup slurping, don't you think?

Ingredients and Materials:

- A full head of cabbage, cut into wedges

- One and a half pounds of lean ground beef

- 4 beef bouillon cubes

- 1 can of diced tomatoes (14.5 ounces)

- 1 can of tomato sauce (8 ounces)

- 2 large carrots, shredded into medium pieces

- 2 tbsp. of white vinegar

- A half-cup of white sugar

- A whole onion, diced small

- 3 cloves of chopped garlic

- 1 1/2 tsp. salt

- A half tsp. of ground black pepper

- About 2 quarts of water

- A large stockpot

Instructions:

1. In a large pot, mix in the diced tomatoes, ground beef, tomato sauce, carrots, onions, and beef cubes.

2. Season the mixture with the salt, pepper, sugar, and vinegar.

3. Pour the water in and bring it to a boil. Stir the mixture from time to time to break up the ground beef and keep it from forming chunks.

4. After bringing the soup to a boil, cover the pot and reduce the heat to simmer.

5. Let it simmer for about half an hour, keeping the heat nice and low.

6. Pour some water into the pot again if needed (is some water has absorbed or boiled off).

7. Add in the cabbage and the garlic. The cabbage will start to get tender after about 25 minutes, and then you're done!

There's nothing easier than throwing in all the ingredients in a pot and simmering, right?

Lamb Loin Chops with Rosemary

You can sear these lamb loin chops on the stove and then in the oven, but you can also grill them if you'd like.

If you have extra time to fire up the barbecue outside, then why not? The lamb loin chops go perfectly well with risotto and can fill you up nicely for the long road trip ahead.

It's certainly a fancier alternative to your basic meat steak, isn't it?

Ingredients and Materials:

- 4 pieces of lamb loin chops with a medium thickness (1.5 inches, 1.25 lbs.)

- 2 tbsp. (about a single fresh stem) of rosemary leaves

- 2 whole cloves of garlic

- 1 tsp. kosher salt

- 1/2 tsp. black pepper (freshly cracked)

- 1 tbsp. extra-virgin olive oil (you can add more oil to oil the skillet when cooking)

- An oven-safe skillet, like a cast-iron skillet

Instructions:

1. Grind the rosemary along with the garlic to create a paste. You can use a mortar and pestle, a knife, or a chopper to grind these ingredients along with the salt and pepper until the mixture becomes a coarse powder.

2. Stir in a tablespoon of the olive oil and mix well to create the rub.

3. After the rub is done, rub it over the lamb loin chops and leave them to marinate at room temp for about half an hour.

4. Heat up your oven to about 400° F. Preheat your oven-safe skillet over medium heat.

5. Coat the skillet's bottom with a thin layer of the olive oil, then sear the lamb chops on it for about four minutes per side.

6. Place the skillet in the oven and cook until the chops reach the desired doneness (rare, medium-rare, well-done, etc.).

Alternatively, you can grill these chops on the barbecue grates or pan-roast them on the grill, too.

The Classic Steak (Serves 2)

Of course, no meat recipe list is complete without the classic steak!

There's no reason you can't enjoy a big, juicy slice of beef while on the road—you need to indulge every now and then.

Who says that fancy steaks are just for upscale restaurants and classy hotels? You won't even need to call in advance and book a reservation for this one! Why waste all that time waiting in line when you can have the perfect steak right in the comfort of your own motor home?

Of course, there are different kinds of rubs that you can make, depending on how you want to enjoy your steak.

You can marinate your steak with a pre-mixed marinade, or spice it up with a dry spice rub. You can also use a paste or a wet rub (olive oil is always a healthier alternative).

This kind of wet rub in this recipe will also work well with chicken if you want to go the poultry route.

Ingredients:

- Two whole boneless ribeye steaks (that's my favorite cut of steak, but you can use whatever type you prefer)

- 2 cloves of minced garlic

- 1 tsp. salt

- 1 tsp. cracked black pepper (of the coarse ground variety)

- 1 tsp. dried thyme

- Extra-virgin olive oil (about one tablespoon)

Instructions:

1. Create the wet rub by combining all of the ingredients and spices together in a small bowl.

2. Make sure that the mixture is mixed smooth enough, then rub the mixture onto each side of the steaks. You can use a spoon to smear the rub properly onto the surface of the steaks.

Afterward, grill it up the way you like it! It definitely doesn't get any easier than that!

Barbecue Sliders

Speaking of classics, the BBQ burger has been around for ages and is definitely here to stay for years to come.

You can make this staple on the road and maybe even throw in a few meatballs in there, too! After all, if you don't want to make them into patties, meatballs work pretty well for those quick, bite-sized snacks when hunger strikes on the road.

They also make for good party picks, just in case you want to have a little mixer while you're on your mobile adventure.

Ingredients and Materials:

- 1 pound of ground beef (always opt for the lean kind)

- Shredded cabbage (you can also use shredded lettuce)

- 1 whole egg

- Half a cup of Japanese bread crumbs

- Half tsp. onion powder

- Slider buns, if you're going for the mini burger route

- Half tsp. salt

- Half tsp. ground pepper

- Half tsp. garlic powder

- A bottle of your favorite barbecue sauce

- A medium-sized mixing bowl

- A whisk

- A mixing spatula

- A slow cooker/crockpot

Instructions:

1. Whisk together the egg, spices, and powders in a medium bowl until the mixture is smooth.

2. Throw in the Japanese bread crumbs and the ground beef using your spatula.

3. When the mixture is blended just right, shape the meat however way you want. You can round them up into little balls if you want to make meatballs, or you can flatten them to form burger patties if you want to make sliders.

4. Then, place the meatballs or patties in the crockpot and pour your fave BBQ sauce over them.

5. Let them cook for about three or four hours on low and serve with shredded veggies on slider buns as you wish!

Beef with Broccoli (Serves 4)

This all-time favorite Chinese recipe is a crowd-pleaser at Chinese restaurants, but who says you need to stop at one to enjoy some beef and broccoli goodness?

Make this delish dish yourself on the road, and it'll be a guaranteed weeknight fave from here on out.

The best thing about this dish is that you can adjust the ratio of the beef to the broccoli if you're a huge fan of the green machine.

You can even add some carrots or red bell peppers for a splash of color.

Ingredients and Materials:

- 2 or 3 stalks of fresh-cut broccoli, chunked into small florets

- 3/4 pound beef sirloin, preferably sliced into thin pieces about an inch long or so depending on your preference

- 2 tbsp. potato starch or corn starch

- 1 tsp. black pepper, freshly ground

- Olive oil or vegetable oil

- 2 tsp. ginger, grated

- 2 whole cloves of garlic, freshly minced

- Optional sesame seeds for garnish

- 2 tbsp. soy sauce

- 1 tsp. sugar

- 1 tsp. sesame oil

- About a cup of water, divided

- A small mixing bowl

- A large skillet

- A colander

Instructions:

1. First, create your sauce mix. Mix the soy sauce, sugar, sesame oil, and about a tablespoon of water. Set aside.

2. In a large skillet, boil some water that's just enough for your ingredients to cook in. You want the ingredients steamed, not boiled.

3. Add the broccoli, then stir from time to time until the florets are cooked - for about 3 minutes.

4. Drain the broccoli using a colander, rinsing them under cool, running water.

5. On a separate plate, mix some black pepper and corn starch together and add your beef slices on top of the mixture.

6. Evenly coat the beef slices on all sides with the starch mixture.

7. Coat the bottom of the skillet with some oil.

8. Heat the thin layer of oil on medium heat, then sauté your beef slices by placing the coated bits one by one into the skillet. Wait until each side is browned nicely, and when they sizzle, transfer them to a clean plate. Be patient. Do the frying in batches and add more oil if needed. Let the beef rest for a while after cooking.

9. Then, stir in the garlic and ginger for about a minute, keep the sauces from the beef in the skillet. Be sure not to let the garlic burn.

10. Toss your broccoli back into the skillet. Reheat for about a minute.

11. Add the beef back into the skillet.

12. Pour the sauce mixture in and stir it well.

13. When everything's cooked well together, transfer your delish dish onto a plate and garnish as you like.

This meal is best served with steamed rice.

Recipes with Chicken

Humans have been enjoying the delicious goodness of poultry since the dawn of time.

Poultry is a good source of protein, vitamins, and minerals.

It can help regulate blood pressure, maintain good cholesterol, and assist you with healthy weight loss, too.

Roast chicken is a family staple, no matter where you are on the road.

It's the perfect Friday night meal for the whole family.

There's nothing quite like the smell of juicy chicken meat roasting in the oven.

You can even make a tradition of it in your motor home, or have it as a quick back-up for when you're hosting guests.

Roast Chicken

It definitely doesn't get more basic than this!

It takes just two minutes of prep time before you pop it inside the oven, but one thing you have to make sure is that you should purchase a high-quality chicken from an organic grocer or your friendly neighborhood butcher to guarantee your poultry's freshness.

Because eating healthy is the name of the game, go for steroid-free, hormone-free, naturally raised, and free-range chickens if you can.

Bear in mind that you also have to check the size of the roasting pan that you own, not to mention the size of your oven itself! You wouldn't want to bring home a nice, juicy chicken only to discover that it won't fit in your roasting pan and rack.

For your oven, make sure that your roasting pan is properly fitted with a good rack, and that this rack is at least an inch above the bottom of your pan.

Make sure you have twine of some sort to help tie the legs together, and some aluminum foil for your chicken.

The size of your chicken will vary and depend greatly on your oven, your roasting pan, your rack, your budget, and the number of people that you will be serving.

Ingredients:

- One whole chicken, approximately 6 pounds

- About a handful of fresh thyme stems and leaves

- Olive oil

- Salt and pepper to taste

Instructions:

1. Before you begin, pre-heat your oven to approximately 425°.

2. For your whole chicken, rinse the meat properly and remove the neck and giblets. Make sure you remove them from inside the cavity. After rinsing your chicken, pat the meat dry using paper towels.

3. With the breast side facing down, drizzle the meat with some olive oil. You can also add salt and pepper and rub it onto the bird to taste.

When you're done handling the chicken, make sure you wash your hands thoroughly as bacteria from raw chicken meat can easily spread onto your kitchen counter, your clothes, your utensils, and so on. It's imperative that you know how to properly handle meat by being safe, clean, and thorough. Nothing ruins a nice meal faster than a really nasty case of tummy aches and vomiting episodes!

4. Place the chicken at the center of the rack in the roasting pan, making sure that the chicken is breast side up.

5. Stuff the chicken cavity with fresh sprigs of thyme. Gather the skin around the cavity and closing it. Make sure you use some sort of twine to tie the legs together.

6. Rub more olive oil over the top of the meat and add more salt and pepper if you desire. You can also garnish your chicken with more thyme leaves if you still have any leftover.

7. Once your oven is hot enough, place the roasting pan inside but do not cover it. Roast the chicken for about an hour and a half.

8. To check if the chicken is done, see if the juices are clear. One option is to try and move the chicken leg a bit to see if it moves freely and easily.

9. When the chicken is done, remove the bird from the oven and tent it with aluminum foil. Let the meat rest for about 15 minutes.

You can also stuff the chicken with many different flavors to experiment with what tastes best. You can use onions, sliced lemons, sage, rosemary, and so much more.

To be honest, you're the master of your own RV kitchen, so you can whip up a nice meal with whatever floats your boat. The beauty of the roasted chicken is that it is so basic and easy to make, which is why there is no limit to the ingredients you can spice it up with.

A meal made with love is always a tasty one, after all!

Leftovers from this basic roast chicken can be used in the chicken soup and in the chicken salad recipes in this section.

Chicken Stir Fry with Sweet Chili

When it comes to easy RV meals that are healthy and delicious at the same time, nothing beats stir fry when you're pressed for time.

Between sautéing and steaming your veggies and meats, you can whip up a delectable and hearty meal in just minutes.

You can use beef, pork, or tofu, but chicken is quintessential. After all, why mess with a classic, right?

Ingredients and Materials:

- 2 pieces of boneless, skinless chicken breasts (a little over 1 pound, total)

- 1 cup of sweet chili sauce

- 1 tbsp. olive oil

- 1 8-ounce can of pineapple bits in juice

- 1 pound fresh broccoli crown (you can also use frozen broccoli if you like)

- Cooked rice based on the instructions on the package

- Some green onions (optional, upon serving for garnish)

- A large pot

- A steamer basket

- A large skillet

Instructions:

1. Chop up the broccoli crown into little florets.

2. In a large pot, add about an inch of water. Using a steaming basket, steam the broccoli. If you don't have a steaming basket, you can add the broccoli directly to the water. Don't forget to cover the pot while steaming, and use medium-high heat.

3. Wait until the water boils, and keep steaming the broccoli florets. When you notice that the broccoli has become tender and has a more vibrant green color (this usually takes about 5 minutes or so), remove the veggies from the heat and set them aside.

4. Now for the chicken! Dice the chicken breasts into little pieces of about an inch in size or so, then season with salt to your liking.

5. Cover a large skillet with a thin layer of cooking oil (about one tablespoon of olive oil) over medium-high heat.

6. Drop in the chicken and stir until the pieces are browned slightly and properly cooked through.

7. Drain the juice from the can of pineapple and add in the pineapple bits.

8. Toss in the sweet chili sauce. Heat the mixture for about 2 minutes.

After that, you're ready to serve! Just add some rice to your plate, and you're good to go.

Pesto Turkey Burger (Serves 4)

Who says you can only make burger patties using beef?

You can go for a poultry alternative using turkey meat as well, and prepping this dish is as easy as 1, 2, 3.

Simple and RV-friendly, these turkey burgers can also be substituted with chicken or even some ground lamb if you have it. The cheesy goodness already provides a lot of the salty taste in this meal, so you won't need to add any additional salt into your recipe, which will lower your sodium intake.

Ingredients and Materials:

- 1 pound ground turkey

- 2 tbsp. pine nuts (obviously, omit if you're allergic!)

- Basil leaves, about 3 stems (fresh is best if you have access to it)

- Black pepper, to taste

- 2 tbsp. extra-virgin olive oil

- 2 or 3 whole cloves of garlic

- Half a cup of freshly-grated parmesan cheese

Instructions:

1. Using a food processor (or whatever tool you have), smoosh the basil leaves, olive oil, pine nuts, garlic, and black pepper together until the mixture is smooth.

2. Mix the ground turkey (or chicken, or ground lamb) along with the parmesan cheese and the basil mixture. Use a wooden spoon or mix it by hand to blend them all together and form patties.

3. Grill the patties if you're having a refreshing barbecue over at a pit stop, or simply fry the patties in a skillet until they're cooked well.

To serve, you can choose to use toasted buns and add in some lettuce and tomatoes for a refreshingly crunchy bite. If you're watching your carb intake, you can substitute the bread for dressed greens.

Classic Chicken Soup

There's a big debate over the effect of chicken soup when helping to keep colds at bay. Whatever the scientific reason behind chicken soup's healing powers, one thing is for sure—it is always a tummy pleaser and a crowd favorite.

Make this recipe during cold and chilly nights when you just want to snuggle inside your RV, sheltered from the weather outside.

Chicken soup works wonders on the body and the mind, relaxing your nerves and calming your emotions. The best part is that chicken soup also freezes well, so your efforts will definitely not go to waste.

Ingredients:

- 1 pound boneless skinless chicken breasts

- A few sprigs of fresh thyme

- 1 bay leaf

- 1-quart chicken broth

- Some olive oil

- About 2 or 3 cloves of garlic

- 10 peppercorns (optional)

- About a cup of sliced carrots

- 1½ cups yellow onion, finely chopped

- 3 stalks of sliced celery

Instructions:

1. Place the chicken breasts in a small saucepan and cover them with chicken broth.

2. Add the peppercorns and thyme. Bring to a boil. Let this chicken stock boil for about ten minutes or so.

3. Coat the bottom of a separate stockpot with a thin layer of olive oil. Throw in the celery, onions, and chopped carrots and stir well.

4. Cook these vegetables over medium heat while stirring, then add the chopped garlic after about 5 minutes.

5. Add the rest of the chicken broth, reduce the heat to low. Simmer this mixture on low heat with the rest of the remaining chicken broth.

6. Remove the chicken breasts from the pan and strain the stock, draining it over your pot of simmering veggies.

7. Shred your chicken into small strips as best as you can and toss them into your simmering

soup pot. Keep simmering until the veggies are tender, then add some more spices like salt, pepper, and thyme to taste.

Chicken Salad with Tarragon

Just like your regular chicken soup, chicken salad is easy, healthy, and perfect for picnics on the road or just a regular weeknight indoors.

If you're serving a crowd, you can easily increase the serving size.

This dish is best served with a little chilled champagne.

You can make this dish with leftover grilled or baked chicken, making good use of leftovers.

Ingredients:

- 3/4 cup mayonnaise

- 4 boneless skinless chicken breast, halved

- Tarragon sprigs (you can add more for optional garnishing afterward)

- Chopped green onions

- 3 stalks of celery, sliced and chopped thinly

- 1-quart chicken broth

- 1 tbsp. white wine vinegar

- Salt and pepper to taste

- A small mixing bowl

- A stockpot or saucepan

- A larger mixing bowl

Instructions:

1. In a small mixing bowl, mix the white wine vinegar and mayonnaise to create a dressing. You can add some salt and pepper depending on your tastes or add some sprigs of fresh tarragon for a revitalizing twist to your regular mayo dressing. Set this aside for later, and get ready to poach your chicken.

2. Place some tarragon sprigs at the bottom of your pot and lay the chicken breast pieces over them.

3. Pour your chicken broth over the chicken, cover your pot, and bring the pot to a boil.

4. Lower the heat to a slow simmer and turn over the chicken breasts, letting them cook for about 10 minutes more or so.

5. When the chicken is properly cooked through, turn off the heat and let the chicken pieces rest inside the pot. Keep the cover of the pot tightly closed for about half an hour more.

6. Transfer the chicken and stock to a fridge-safe, airtight container (like a glass Pyrex dish) and chill the chicken.

7. When you're ready to make your salad, take out the chicken breasts and keep the stock for future use. The number of ways you can reuse chicken stock is endless (stock can also be frozen). Don't forget to discard the tarragon sprigs.

8. As for your chicken, chop it into small pieces or shred it into a large bowl.

9. Toss in your dressing, green onions, and celery, then stir. Coat the chicken completely.

You can opt to garnish the salad with some fresh tarragon or even some slivered almonds for extra crunch.

Serve the chicken salad over a lettuce leaf "plate," or serve it in a bun sandwich. This chicken salad is best served chilled.

Vegetarian Dishes

If you think that being on the road all the time limits your vegetarian choices, think again!

Despite the strict limits of a vegetarian meal, you can still enjoy a hearty dish without resorting to instant meals and takeaway boxes at pit stops and fast food joints. You can work a little magic in your RV kitchen to please even the pickiest of tastes.

Potato Tacos (8 Servings)

Easy and filling at the same time, potato tacos are a vegetarian twist to beef tacos and other meaty variants out there.

You can opt to bake the potatoes the night before to save yourself some time in the kitchen. Add to the delectable taste of the tacos with some shredded cheddar cheese or some queso fresco that's crumbled.

This recipe is extremely versatile and appeases even the pickiest eaters.

You can use flour or corn tortillas. Add any number of toppings to suit your tastes.

Ingredients:

- 1 tsp. ground coriander

- 1 tsp. ground cumin

- 1 tsp. dried oregano

- Half a teaspoon of salt

- 2 tsp. chili powder

- 1 tsp. corn starch

- ¼ tsp. ground black pepper

- Large yellow onion, halved, diced and chopped

- About one or two tbsp. olive oil or other cooking oil

- 1 seeded bell pepper, chopped

- 2-3 whole cloves of minced garlic

- A sliced jalapeno pepper without seeds and pith (optional)

- 1½ pounds potatoes, unpeeled, quartered (you can bake them the night before)

- Flour or corn tortillas

For your toppings, you can add numerous spices and veggies—the more colorful they are, the better!

Some suggested toppings include:

- Shredded cabbage

- Shredded lettuce

- Chopped cilantro

- Avocado slices

- Guacamole

- Diced tomatoes

- Wedges of fresh lime

- Hot sauce

- Salsa

- Sour cream

Instructions:

1. In a large skillet, heat the oil over medium heat.

2. Add the peppers, onions, and garlic and stir well. Sauté the veggies for about 3 minutes or so, checking to see if they're soft and browned.

3. Toss in the sliced potatoes and cook for another minute.

4. Mix the spices together in a separate, small mixing bowl.

5. Sprinkle the mixture of spices over the veggies and stir until your potatoes are evenly coated.

6. Crank up the heat to medium-high, then keep stirring and sautéing for about 4 minutes more.

7. Remove the skillet from the heat and scoop the filling onto warmed tortillas.

Jalapeno Pizza Rollups

If you're looking for an RV-friendly vegetarian meal with all the sinful goodness of actual pizza, look no further!

With only 4 basic ingredients and a heat level you can totally control, these pizza rollups are light and easy in the calorie department and have a nice little kick.

Ingredients:

- Pizza dough, good for one whole pizza (store-bought or home-made, your choice)

- 1 can green chilies, diced, drained (4 ounces)

- 1 can jalapenos, diced, drained (4 ounces)

- 1 cup shredded mozzarella cheese

Instructions:

1. Press the pizza dough or roll it onto a floured surface, approximately 10 x 12 inches in size.

2. Drain the can of chilies and dice them. Dice the jalapenos.

3. When you're satisfied with the size of your dough, sprinkle the green chilies all over. Make

sure that you set aside an edge at the top of the long side of the dough at about an inch in size.

4. Sprinkle the diced jalapenos as well, adjusting the amount based on how hot you want the pizza rollups to be.

5. Top the dough with some grated cheese, keeping in mind the topping-free inch on the edge of the dough.

6. And now for the rollups! Starting with the long edge of the dough that's facing you, roll the dough and end with the unfilled edge, pressing the dough tightly and firmly to seal it completely.

7. Chill the roll in the fridge for about an hour, because chilling the roll will make it easier for you to slice it.

8. With the roll chilled, cut the roll into slices of about ¾ of an inch wide.

9. Lay these slices on a baking sheet lined with parchment paper. You can also use an oiled

baking sheet depending on the tools you have available.

10. Let the slices rest at room temp for about half an hour. This will allow the rolls to rise a little bit and puff up.

11. While waiting, heat your oven to 425°.

12. Bake the rolls for 15 minutes or until they're browned and bubbling.

Linguini with Shallots, Mushrooms

A veggie dish that's both hearty and yummy, this linguini meal with caramelized shallots is a guaranteed burst of flavors in your mouth that'll leave you wanting for more long after the last bite.

You can opt to use whole wheat linguini to go easy on the sugar, and skip the salt altogether if the cheese is enough for you.

Go ahead and adjust the way you want to!

Ingredients:

- Dried linguini (you can also use spaghetti), 6 ounces, cooked based on the directions on the package

- Half a cup of water, leftover from after cooking the pasta

- Half a cup (about one piece) large finely minced shallot

- 12 chopped sage leaves

- Extra virgin olive oil

- 2 cups crimini mushrooms, chopped

- Salt and pepper to taste

- 1/4 cup parmesan cheese, freshly grated

- A pot large enough for pasta and water

- A colander to strain the pasta

- A medium to large skillet

Instructions:

1. Cook the pasta according to the directions on the package.

2. While you're cooking the pasta, coat the bottom of a medium skillet with olive oil and heat over medium heat.

3. Sauté the shallots and stir until they turn a golden brown color. This usually takes about 15 minutes or so.

4. Add the sage to the skillet with the shallots and let the oil completely coat the chopped bits for about a minute.

5. Toss the mushrooms into the shallots and sage and cook for about 8 minutes. If you feel like the mixture is too dry, you can add more olive oil and cook until the mushrooms until they turn golden brown and become soft. Add some salt and pepper to taste.

6. Your pasta should be done by now, so drain it and keep about half a cup of the pasta water.

7. Toss the mushroom mix and the pasta together, using the salted water as an added ingredient if the sauce seems a tad too dry.

Serve on plates and top with cheese as desired.

Delicious Lasagna

One of the easiest yet healthiest RV-friendly budget meals, this vegetarian lasagna is rich and filling but very conscious about fat intake.

This savory meal is easy on the cholesterol levels but generous with the flavor, and it's bound to be a family fave even for the kids.

Ingredients:

- Fat-free cottage cheese (16 ounces, whole carton)

- An 8-ounce package of frozen artichoke hearts, thawed and chopped

- A 10-ounce package of frozen spinach, thawed and gently squeezed dry

- 3 stems of chopped fresh basil

- 8 sheets of "oven-ready" no-boil lasagna noodles

- Marinara sauce (26 ounces)

- 4 tbsp. parmesan cheese, freshly grated

- Half a teaspoon of salt

- Pepper to taste

- An 8x8 baking dish

- A mixing bowl

Instructions:

1. Preheat the oven to 350°.

2. Lightly oil the bottom and sides of the baking dish.

3. Mix the spinach, basil, artichoke hearts, salt, and pepper in a medium bowl. Blend the mixture well with a fork to keep the spinach from bunching up together. Then, add the cottage cheese and blend well.

4. Pour just enough marinara sauce to cover the bottom of the dish completely.

5. Lay two sheets of lasagna noodles on top of the marinara sauce layer.

6. Add a third of the cheese mixture evenly over the noodles.

7. Place another two sheets of pasta over the mixture, then the cheese mixture in the same amount evenly over the surface.

8. Next, add the final layer and top with the rest of the cheese mixture.

9. Pour the rest of the pasta sauce over the lasagna, making sure to coat the very top layer. It's okay to let the sauce drip down deliciously on the sides of the stacked layers.

10. Finally, sprinkle the parmesan generously over the top and bake for about 45 minutes.

11. When the pasta is nicely browned, it's ready. Remove it from the oven and let it rest for about 10 minutes before digging in!

Vegetarian Mapo Tofu

Here's a wonderful Asian dish that's warm and welcome on a chilly weeknight.

Spicy and salty in all the right amounts, this tofu dish is traditionally cooked with some ground beef or ground pork, but with this vegetarian variation, you can use tofu instead of meat, and it will be just as delectable.

A special condiment that will definitely perk up your tofu dish is the chili bean sauce, something that you can find in your nearest Asian grocer.

This chili bean paste consists of fermented soybeans, salted chili peppers, garlic, sugar, and a medley of other flavorful spices.

When shopping for your tofu, do not use the Japanese silken style tofu as it will be too soft and might easily fall apart when used in this recipe.

Ingredients:

- One pound of medium firmness tofu, cut into bite-sized cubes

- 3 tbsp. olive oil

- Spices:

    o 1 tbsp. fresh, grated ginger

    o Half a teaspoon of ground Sichuan peppercorns

    o 3 whole cloves of garlic, minced

    o Green onions, minced, white parts

- o 2 tbsp. chili bean paste

- o A quarter cup of water and dry sherry

- o 2 tsp. corn starch

- o ½ tsp. sugar

- o 2 tbsp. low sodium soy sauce

- o 2 tsp. sesame oil

- Garnish:

  - o Green parts of green onions, sliced

- A heat-safe bowl

- About 3 cups of water

- A large skillet or wok

Instructions:

1. Boil the water.

2. Place the cubed tofu in the heat-safe bowl and pour the boiling water over it to completely cover the tofu. Leave the tofu uncovered and resting in the boiling water.

3. Coat the bottom of a large skillet or wok with a thin layer of olive oil and heat the wok or skillet over medium heat.

4. Toss in the spices (garlic, ginger, Sichuan peppercorns, minced green onions) and constantly stir, letting the veggies wilt and allowing the garlic and onions to turn a nice shade of golden brown. This usually takes about 3 minutes.

5. Mix in the chili bean paste and lower the temp.

6. Drain your tofu and slide it into the wok. Toss it as gently as you can and add the rest of the spices and sauces over the tofu.

7. Make sure the tofu is fully coated as you stir every now and then. Let the sauce simmer. It will thicken in about a minute or two.

Serve and garnish as you like. Enjoy it over a cup of steamed rice.

Vegan Recipes

The common misconception is that vegan recipes are more restricted and extremely limited compared to non-vegan ones, but all it really takes is a little creativity and just knowing where to look.

You can enjoy regular vegan meals and stick to your healthy diet (not to mention stick to your wallet-friendly budget too!) with these fool-proof vegan recipes you can whip up in a jiffy while you're on the road.

Now, while plenty of vegan recipes call for a chicken broth substitute, this doesn't necessarily mean that you need to forego your cruelty-free preferences and sacrifice your principles all for a good meal.

You can still enjoy chicken broth-esque recipes with approved plant-based substitutes. Don't buy into the misconception that plant-based substitutes lack the depth of flavor that you can get from real chicken broth.

Soups, pilaffs, stews, and bean recipes can be fully vegan while maintaining the same kind of stellar delectable flavor found in chicken stock with alternatives that contain oregano, garlic, thyme, carrots, celery, and onions.

When it comes to pasta, you can also go for vegan alternatives as long as you carefully inspect the package ingredients. Avoid fresh kinds of pasta that may have egg in them and go for plant-based ingredients such as semolina and enriched wheat flour.

Tomato Florentine Soup (Serves 6)

Classic tomato soup never fails to bring comfort and warmth on any given day. Have your chicken broth substitute on hand and always in stock in your pantry.

Open yourself up to a wealth of flavors and a variety of recipes without sacrificing taste and your animal-free preferences.

Ingredients:

- 14.5-ounce chicken broth substitute of your choice

- 1 tbsp. brown sugar

- A pinch or so of ground nutmeg

- 10 ounces frozen chopped spinach

- 14.5 ounce can of stewed tomatoes, chopped

- 12 fluid ounce can of tomato-vegetable juice cocktail

- 10.75 ounce condensed tomato soup (about one can)

- salt and ground black pepper to taste

- Half a cup of cooked macaroni

- A saucepan

- A whisk

Instructions:

1. In a saucepan, use a wire whisk to mix in the tomatoes, juice, broth, and condensed tomato soup over medium heat.

2. Add the frozen spinach along with the nutmeg, sugar, salt, and pepper.

3. Cook this mixture on medium-low heat, for about 20 minutes, until the spinach has become tender. Be careful not to let the mixture boil.

4. Throw in the cooked pasta and simmer for another 10 minutes before serving.

Pasta Arrabbiata (Serves 6)

Here's another classic pasta dish that's easy to prepare and incredibly affordable. This dish is quick to prepare, as the cooking time is just about the same as the time it takes to boil the water.

It's a two-pot meal and perfect for the limited space inside your RV. Penne is good, but you can always change it up and try any kind of pasta you like.

This lightly sauced meal is meat-free and dairy-free, so it's the healthiest, simplest dish ever!

Ingredients:

- 1 pound dried pasta of your choice

- 1/3 cup extra-virgin olive oil

- 1 cup yellow onion, chopped finely

- 4-6 cloves of minced garlic

- Kosher salt to taste, as well as some fresh Italian parsley leaves or fresh basil to garnish

- 1 to 3 tsp. dried red chili flakes

- 26 to 28 ounces of canned tomatoes (about 3 cups, crushed or diced)

Instructions:

1. Coat the bottom of a large saucepan over medium heat with olive oil.

2. Throw in the chopped onion, constantly stirring, waiting until the onions are soft. This takes about five minutes.

102

3. When the chopped onions are soft but aren't browned just yet, add the garlic bits and lower the heat slightly, stirring constantly. Cook until the onion begins to brown, but be careful not to let them burn.

4. Sprinkle the dried red chili flakes into the pot and keep stirring for another minute.

5. Mix in the crushed tomatoes and let them simmer for about 10-15 minutes more.

6. At this time, you should cook the pasta according to the instructions on the package.

7. Drain the pasta and pour the sauce over it generously. Serve and enjoy!

Avocado Wraps With Hummus

Simple and fresh, there's just something revitalizing about avocado that's hard to describe.

While you're RV-ing the days away, it's always a good idea to munch on some fresh wraps or even head out for a lovely picnic on a bright and sunny day.

With this dish, you won't even have to fire up the stove or make use of your kitchen. All you really need is fresh greens, and you're good to go.

Sometimes, the simplest things are the most rewarding, don't you think?

Ingredients (per wrap):

- Tortilla, wrap, or flatbread

- 3 tbsp. of hummus

- About half an avocado

- Half a tomato, sliced

- Minced garlic to taste

- Leafy greens of your choice

- Salt and pepper to taste

Instructions:

There's really nothing easier, quicker, healthier, and more affordable than this recipe!

1. Lay out the tortilla wraps or flatbread and spread the hummus generously over the surface as you like.

2. Make sure that the minced garlic has no extra juice, then sprinkle the garlic over the hummus, along with some salt and pepper to taste.

3. Place about a handful or so of your choice of leafy greens over your hummus.

4. Spread the avocado over the surface of the greens, add in more leafy greens over the layer as needed, then top with tomatoes slices however way you want it.

5. Roll, fold, and munch away!

You can serve as many wraps as you want. It makes for a quick fix when your tummy's grumbling, or when you need a fast and easy way to entertain some newfound friends you met at the campground!

Black Bean Soup

Do you have a bad case of the munchies? Sometimes, feeling hungry is exactly that—a feeling.

It's best to curb these unhealthy cravings with real, actual food—but sometimes, when you're hungry, you're really hungry!

To fight off those hunger pains, indulge in some healthy boosts of protein with black beans—and couple that with some heart-healthy fiber too!

Ingredients:

- 4 cans of 15-ounces each black beans (you can also go for 6 cups cooked black beans)

- 1 finely chopped onion

- ¼ cup finely chopped fresh cilantro

- Lime juice

- 1 clove of minced garlic

- 1 tbsp. olive oil

- 1 tsp. chili powder

- Salt and pepper to taste

- 1 cup of water

- Blender or food processor

- A saucepan

Instructions:

1. Blend one cup of water with the beans in a blender or a food processor. Blend until the puree is chunky

2. In a pot on medium-high heat, add the tablespoon of olive oil, garlic, and onions.

3. Sauté the garlic and onions for about a minute or two until the onions are translucent.

4. Mix in the bean mixture into the pot.

5. Add the cilantro, lime juice, chili powder, salt, and cayenne.

6. Let the soup simmer for a few minutes, making sure not to let the soup dry too much before you serve it.

Black Pepper Tofu (Serves 4)

There is truly no limit to the wonders of tofu!

Made from soybean curds, this naturally gluten-free dish is low in calories and a nutritious source of iron and calcium. It does not contain cholesterol, and for vegans and vegetarians, it is an excellent source of protein.

For your own well-being, tofu can help lower the risk of diabetes, heart disease, and obesity. It can help boost energy, enhance your hair, and even benefit your skin!

Ingredients:

- 4 tbsp. water

- 1 tbsp. cornstarch

- A brick of tofu, extra firm, 14 to 16 ounces

- 4 tbsp. soy sauce

- 1 tbsp. ginger root, freshly grated

- 2 to 4 tsp. ground black pepper

- 1 tbsp. rice wine, dry sherry, or water

- 1 tbsp. rice vinegar

- 1 red bell pepper, thinly sliced

- 1 tsp. sugar

- 3 tbsp. olive oil

- Slivered green onion as an optional garnish

- Zip-top plastic bag, gallon size

Instructions:

1. Cut up the brick of tofu into bite-size cubes.

2. Add the tofu to the zip-top plastic bag.

3. In a small bowl, mix the corn starch, soy sauce, ginger root, water, sherry, rice vinegar, sugar, and black pepper. Mix it well, then pour the mixture into the tofu in the plastic bag.

4. Carefully shake the sealed plastic bag until the tofu is fully covered. Let the tofu marinate in the fridge. You can leave it in the fridge for up to 24 hours, but give it at least one hour to marinate.

5. When you're ready to cook the tofu, use a strainer over a bowl to drain the tofu, saving the marinade for later.

6. As you let the tofu rest on the strainer, heat a large skillet or a wok over high heat. Coat the

bottom of the pan with some oil, then stir in and cook the slivered red pepper for about a minute.

7. Stir fry or sauté the strained tofu into the pan for about 5 to 10 minutes, until the tofu cubes turn brown. Keep tossing the cubes every so often.

8. Add the marinade that you set aside into the pan. Stir the contents to coat the tofu, and lower the heat to medium.

9. After about a minute or so as you continue to stir, the sauce should thicken.

You are now ready to serve! Once on the plate, you can choose to garnish the dish with some slivered green onions if you like.

This dish is also best enjoyed with some steamed rice.

Moroccan Stew - Nice and Spicy!
(Serves 4)

Sometimes, your family's mood can call for some spicy dishes, especially during cool evenings indoors.

You can adjust the Moroccan spices as necessary, and dial in the heat depending on your palate.

Speaking of spicy food, did you know that consuming spicy dishes about once every day can help lower mortality rates? These longevity benefits were studied by Harvard and the China National Center for Disease Control and Prevention in 2015.

Spicy foods help speed up your metabolism and can slow down your appetite if you don't want to overeat. Spices like curcumin, ginger, and garlic have amazing anti-inflammatory effects as well.

Turmeric and cumin are antioxidant powerhouses with great antimicrobial properties. Don't be afraid to spice things up!

Ingredients:

- 1 tsp. ground cumin

- 1 tsp. ground paprika

- 1 tsp. ground coriander

- 1 tsp. kosher salt

- 1 tsp. black pepper

- 2 tbsp. extra virgin olive oil

- Half a teaspoon of cayenne pepper

- 1 can garbanzo beans (15 ounces) or chickpeas, drained and rinsed

- 1 chopped medium onion

- 2 minced cloves of garlic

- 1 chopped red pepper

- 1 large russet potato (peeled and cubed)

- 2 cups of cauliflower florets

- 2 cups of vegetable stock

- Optional: chopped parsley or cilantro as garnish

- Saucepan with a lid

- Small mixing bowl

Instructions:

1. Coat the bottom of your pan with olive oil, and heat over medium heat (make sure you have a tight-fitting lid).

2. Throw in the chopped onion. Sauté the onions until they're soft, for about 3-4 minutes.

3. Add the red pepper and garlic and stir. Be careful not to let the garlic burn. Cook for about 2 or 3 minutes.

4. Mix your spices together and set aside in a small bowl. Throw the spices in and sprinkle on the contents of the pan. Stir to coat and mix properly.

5. Pour in the stock.

6. Add the potatoes cubes. Cover the pan and bring to a boil.

7. After about ten minutes, check if the potatoes are tender when poked with a fork.

8. Reduce the heat to a simmer, then add the beans and the cauliflower florets. Stir and cover for about ten more minutes.

Seafood Dishes

Sure, you've got your typical leafy green salads when you think about healthy eats, but what about a different take this time?

From greasy fries to oily chips, there's no limit to the sinful wonders of the potato. Potatoes can be healthy if you know how to prep them correctly.

Potato Salad with Shrimp

Here's a fresh and seafood-based twist to your classic potato salad.

It's light, healthy, and the perfect appetizer or pre-meal snack for when your tummy is grumbling on the road.

Ingredients and Materials:

- 10 large potatoes, washed and scrubbed well (peeling is optional)

- Chopped green onions

- Chopped dill pickles

- 12 whole eggs

- 2 cups (low-fat) mayonnaise

- 2 tbsp. celery salt

- 2 tbsp. paprika

- A single can of 4-ounce shrimp

- A single can of 4-ounce drained small shrimp

- Salt and pepper to taste

- Two large pots or saucepans

- A large mixing bowl

- At least one mixing spoon

Instructions:

1. In a large pot, place your big baking potatoes and cover the pot with water.

2. Boil the potatoes, until you start to feel them softening.

3. When the baking potatoes are soft, take them out of the water and set them aside to cool.

4. After the potatoes are cool enough to handle, peel the potatoes and chop them up into bite-sized pieces.

5. Separately, put your eggs in a large saucepan and cover them completely with water. Bring the water to a boil.

6. Boil the eggs in the water for about a minute or so.

7. Cover the saucepan and remove it from the heat. Let the eggs stand in the hot water.

8. After about 10-12 minutes, remove the eggs from the hot water.

9. Allow the eggs to cool before you peel them and chop them up.

10. In a large mixing bowl, mix the potatoes, eggs, dill pickles, green onions, and cans of shrimp together.

11. Mix in the celery salt, paprika, and the low-fat mayonnaise.

12. When everything is mixed well, season the salad with ground black pepper and some salt.

13. Chill the salad in the fridge for at least two hours before serving. Serve chilled.

Tuna Cakes (makes 6-8)

Canned or packaged tuna is a staple for your RV kitchen. Here's a recipe for making canned tuna in a different way, rather than just the boring tuna sandwich on white bread.

Ingredients:

- 2 eggs

- 2 tsp lemon juice

- 4 tbsp. parmesan cheese

- ½ cup of seasoned bread crumbs

- A total of about 15 ounces of chunk light tuna in water (drained cans or pouches)

- 2 tbsp diced white onion

- Black pepper to taste

- Salt to taste

- Olive oil or cooking oil of choice

- Medium mixing bowl

- A skillet

Instructions:

1. Beat the eggs and lemon juice in a bowl.

2. Stir in the parmesan cheese and bread crumbs.

3. Fold in the tuna and onion until it's all well-mixed.

4. Season with salt and pepper.

5. Shape the tuna mixture into 1-inch-thick patties.

6. Heat the oil in a skillet over medium heat.

7. Fry the tuna patties until they're golden brown, about 5 minutes per side.

Serve with a veggie of choice and slices of lemon for garnish.

Desserts

There is definitely no complete meal without dessert.

While the common misconception is that desserts are usually unhealthy, they can actually be less sinful and easy to make if you know how to prep them properly.

It's always a good idea to leave room for dessert so that you can indulge after a hearty meal.

Classic Ice Cream

Ice cream is a dessert staple, no matter where you are in the world.

Go for homemade ice cream so that you can control the ingredients that you put into your dish. The freshest ingredients coupled with affordable, heart-healthy goodies make your regular ice cream an even bigger kitchen fave.

Ingredients:

- 1 tbsp. vanilla

- 3 egg yolks

- 3 cups divided half & half

- 3/4 cup sugar

- 1/8 tsp. sea salt

- A medium saucepan

- A small mixing bowl

Instructions:

1. Stir the sugar, salt, and two cups of the half & half in a medium saucepan. Make sure to

combine them completely so that the salt and the sugar are dissolved well.

2. Cook the pan over medium heat, careful not to let the mixture boil.

3. Remove the pan from the heat.

4. In a separate small bowl, whisk the egg yolks until they are smooth then mix the remaining cup of half & half. Stir and blend well.

5. Pour your egg mixture slowly into the pan. Make sure you constantly whisk the mixture into the warm half & half mixture.

6. Return the saucepan to medium heat. Use a wooden spoon to stir it constantly, doing so until the base of the ice cream thickens.

7. Keep doing this until the ice cream base starts to coat the back of the spoon. Make sure you don't let the mixture boil.

8. Remove the pot from the heat, but keep stirring for about 2 or 3 minutes more.

9. With a sieve, strain the ice cream base into a bowl. Cover it well.

10. Let the mixture cool overnight in the fridge. Once the ice cream is chilled, add the vanilla and stir.

11. Using an ice cream processor, transfer the mixture into a freezer-safe container and freeze until it's ready to eat!

Yogurt Parfait

Here's a healthier alternative to your basic ice cream, making for a deliciously sweet treat without the guilt.

Ingredients:

- 3 cups vanilla nonfat yogurt

- 1 cup of granola

- 1 cup frozen strawberries in juice (fresh or defrosted)

- 1 pint fresh blackberries or blueberries

Instructions:

1. Defrost the frozen berries and combine them with the fresh berries (you can also use fresh raspberries if you like).

2. Use about 4 tall glasses and layer about a third cup of vanilla yogurt onto the bottom.

3. Layer the fruit and the granola alternately until you fill up your glasses to the top.

4. To keep the granola nice and crunchy, serve while fresh!

Leche Flan

What is leche flan? Does it sound mysteriously exotic?

As one of the tastiest traditional desserts in the Philippines, leche flan is a simple dish that's an explosion of gastronomic delights in itself.

The flan may be made up to one day in advance.

Ingredients:

- 1/4 cup water

- 1/2 cup sugar

- 3 large eggs

- One and a half cups of half & half

- 1 tbsp. vanilla

- 1 can condensed milk (sweetened, 14 ounces approximately)

- A saucepan

- A large mixing bowl

- A whisk

- Pie pan or custard dishes

Instructions:

1. Heat your oven to about 325°.

2. In some custard dishes or a pie pan, oil them lightly with olive oil.

3. In a saucepan, mix the sugar and water together. Boil this slowly until this mixture turns into a golden caramel hue, which takes about a little more than five minutes.

4. When it turns into a nice brown caramel, remove it from the heat.

5. Pour the caramel carefully into the pie pan that's been oiled. Swirl the mixture until you coat the bottom and line a little bit of the sides.

6. In a large bowl, use a wire whisk to beat the eggs well until the mixture is smooth, mixing in the sweetened condensed milk in the process.

7. Whisk in the vanilla and the half & half.

8. Pour the egg mixture over the caramel, and bake it in a water bath for about half an hour.

9. Once the custard sets, it should still jiggle a little once the mixture cools down.

10. Let it cool on a rack for about half an hour, then cover with plastic wrap and set it in the fridge for a day in advance.

When you're ready to serve, use a thin knife and run it along the edge of the pan to loosen the flan a bit. Then, invert the flan onto a plate and serve!

Rosemary and Lemon Olive Oil Cake

The idea of an olive oil cake might sound odd, but it's one of the easiest and healthiest dessert recipes you will ever have the pleasure of making.

You can also use some fresh strawberries or fresh raspberries and serve this at room temp with some additional toppings.

Ingredients:

- 2 whole eggs

- 2 cups all-purpose white flour

- 3/4 cup sugar

- 1 tsp. salt

- 1 tbsp. baking powder

- 1 cup buttermilk

- 3/4 cup olive oil plus some to oil the pan

- 2 tbsp. rosemary (fresh, minced finely, should be about two stems or so; you can also have some extra for garnishing if desired)

- One lemon, for the juice and the zest (approximately 4tbsp.)

- A mixing bowl

- A springform baking pan

- A baking sheet

- Whisk, hand-beater, or electric mixer

Instructions:

1. Preheat your oven to about 350°.

2. Coat the bottom of a springform pan with oil.

3. Place this pan on a baking sheet.

4. Sift the flour together with the salt and the baking powder, then set this aside.

5. Place the sugar, eggs, and olive oil in a mixing bowl and beat for about two minutes. Do so until the mixture is combined well until it is nice and fluffy.

6. Stir and combine the lemon zest, juice, and the buttermilk. Keep beating the mixture of flour until it is blended well.

7. Mix the minced rosemary and combine well.

8. Pour the batter into your prepped pan. If you have more rosemary left, sprinkle a few minced pieces over the top of the batter decoratively.

9. Bake your pan in the oven for about 40 to 45 minutes, then remove it from the wire rack.

Let the pan rest for about 5 minutes and cool it well. This can be prepped a day in advance before serving.

Traditional Apple Pie

Of course, when we talk about making dessert for the whole family, we can't forget about America's favorite dessert.

Traditional apple pie is a sure winner for all groups, whether you're on the road or not.

Ingredients:

- Any kind of your favorite refrigerated pie crust

- Butter to brush on the crust

- A quarter cup of orange juice (or lemon juice)

- 2 tbsp. tapioca flour or corn starch

- 1 cup of sugar

- 7-8 golden apples, cut into pieces

- 1 tsp. cinnamon

- Nutmeg and salt to taste

- Pie pan

- 2 mixing bowls

Instructions:

1. Preheat your oven to 350 degrees.

2. Line the bottom of your pan with pie crust and brush the pie crust with some melted butter.

3. In a separate bowl, add the citrus juice. Core, peel, and slice the apples and place them inside the bowl with the citrus juice, stirring well.

4. In another small bowl, mix the corn starch or tapioca flour, salt, spices, and sugar.

5. Combine this sugar mixture with the juice and apples. Toss and stir well to coat properly.

6. Pour the apple mixture into your pie pan. You can also add more butter if desired.

7. Top the pie with the second layer of crust and crimp the edges to seal the pie.

8. With a tablespoon of water, whisk together one egg and brush this egg mixture over your crust.

9. Then, you can sprinkle the top of the pie with some cinnamon or sugar if you want

10. Bake for about 70 minutes until ready!

Vegan Cheesecake

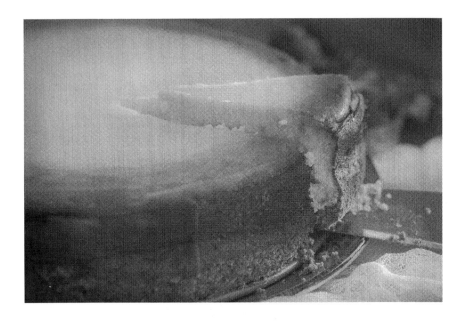

Who says desserts have to be sinful all the time?

Vegans have plenty of delectable animal byproduct-free options when it comes to delectable desserts.

This vegan cheesecake uses coconut cream in its filling and forgoes eggs and cream for tofu and nuts. It also skips the butter in favor of coconut oil.

Ingredients:

- 8 ounces tofu, silken

- 1 cup coconut cream

- One and a half cup of macadamia nuts or raw cashews

- 1 tbsp. corn starch

- ¾ cup sugar

- ⅛ tsp. salt

- 2 tsp. pure vanilla extract

- 2 tsp. lemon zest

- 1 tbsp. lemon juice

- 1 cup oat flour (gluten-free)

- 1 cup toasted pecans

- 3 tbsp. pure maple syrup

- ½ tsp. salt

- ⅓ cup melted coconut oil

Instructions:

1. In a medium heatproof bowl, place your cashew nuts or macadamia nuts and cover the heatproof bowl with boiling water. Make sure the water is about an inch in depth and let the nuts soak for about an hour.

2. Preheat the oven to 350°F. Use cooking spray to coat a 9-inch springform pan.

3. For your crust, use a food processor and ground the pecans finely.

4. Combine coconut oil, maple syrup, oat flour, and salt into the food processor with the pecans.

Press this firmly onto the bottom of the pan that you prepared.

5. For approximately 15 minutes, bake the crust until it's set (make sure that it is not browned yet).

6. Use a wire rack and let it cool for another 15 minutes.

7. Drain your chosen nuts. Transfer them into a food processor or a blender, and mix in the coconut cream, tofu, vanilla, lemon zest, sugar, salt, and corn starch. Blend these ingredients until they are smooth.

8. Scrape them into the crust. Carefully place the cheesecake onto a baking sheet.

9. Bake the cheesecake until the edges start to turn a little dry. Check to see if the center looks a bit

jiggly. This should take about 50 minutes to an hour.

10. When done, cool it on a wire rack at room temperature for another hour. When you place it inside the fridge, make sure that it's uncovered.

11. Chill it for about 3 hours.

12. When you're ready to eat, run a sharp knife around the sides to loosen the edges, then serve.

Final Tips and Tricks

Aside from knowing how to plan and cook your own meals for a healthier and more affordable RV life, here are just a few more final tips and tricks to help you cut down on your expenses while living on the road.

After all, if you're well within budget and not worrying about finances all the time, this will definitely make you less stressed out on the road.

Fantastic Freebies

When you find a free spot, try to park as often as you can. There are a lot of free RV spots you can check across the country.

Many apps are available to help you scout the best one out there. Online sources like FreeCampsites.net can assist you with looking for free spots to park as well, so know how to maximize the information online and save on gas at the same time.

Solar Saves

Why not make the most of the sunlight while you're outdoors anyway?

Try and invest in RV solar panels if you can. This will not only help you cut back on your electricity, but it will also help you do your part for Mother Nature with using a renewable energy source.

Club Colleagues

There are tons of RV memberships in the industry, and if you know how to make the most of them, you can score discounted campground fees and RV park rates.

Extended stays will also help you take advantage of these discounts, as well as help you save on gas. Plus, having a community you belong to can really come in handy when you're in a pinch.

You can always turn to a network of people who have gone through or are going through the same thing as you are, and can assist you with your concerns no matter where you are in the country.

They can also readily lend a hand in case you are ever near their area—think of it as expanding your web of communications and friends!

Budget Bound

Be aware of your budget and stick to it.

A lot of groups who start RV-ing feel like the freedom on the road equates to freely spending on anything and everything.

It can be pretty tempting to indulge when you don't have a strict schedule to follow, but managing your finances well is key in supporting a healthy and happy RV lifestyle.

Make sure you adopt a strict budgeting habit if you don't want your RV life to be cut short.

Compact Choices

If you have the choice, pick a smaller vehicle. The bigger your motor home, the bigger your costs will be.

A smaller vehicle also helps you save up on gas considerably. Know how to determine excess and how to live minimally.

Make it Minimal

Know what your priorities are.

- What do you imagine your RV life looks like?

- What will be your sources of income, and what are the most important factors in your lifestyle on the road?

- What can you live without, and what are the bare essentials that will make you happy?

Knowing these things can help you make sound decisions and let you know how you can prioritize your wants versus your needs and how you can decide on what you can do without.

Plan, Plan, Plan

Stick to a plan. When you have a plan, you know exactly where you want and need to go.

You don't waste gas and valuable resources running around in circles without a definite destination. This not only wastes gas, but it also wastes food!

Imagine going round and round and getting hungry all the time in between—plus, you definitely wouldn't want to run out of food in the middle of nowhere in case you get lost!

Invest in some GPS tools so that you can easily find your way around no matter where you end up.

Boondock Basics

Lots of RV-ers boondock whenever possible.

You can try overnight stops at free places like Lowe's, Cabela's, Walmart, Cracker Barrel, or Home Depot.

If you're going to be camping for longer periods of time, you can try BLM (Bureau of Land Management) lands or state forests. Just make sure that you check ahead of time if it's legal to park overnight in your campground of choice.

Maintenance Mishaps

When you can, try to maintain your RV as often as possible.

Check your tire pressure. Under filled or overfilled tires will cause you a lot of stress and money when things go wrong.

Be diligent when it comes to these maintenance musts—remember, always prioritize safety first!

Speaking of safety and maintenance, make sure you have some extended warranty on your RV. It never hurts to have more coverage when you're going on a long trip.

You should also carry a few basic tools with you in case of emergencies when something breaks down. You can fix the minor issues when you can, but it's always best to call a professional, or you might end up making things worse and racking up more and more fees on repairs.

Insurance Insecurity

Having good health insurance ensures cheaper medical costs in case of untoward accidents and health problems due to inclement weather and the like.

Because you are on the road all the time, it helps to be prepared for anything you might encounter—and that includes viruses and bacteria whenever you are exposed to the elements.

Carry appropriate car and RV insurance on your vehicles. Because you're on the road constantly as a lifestyle, you'll want good coverage.

Lingering Leftovers

When you're cooking, whip up extra batches and double your volume if you can. When you have plenty of leftovers, freeze them and store them for a rainy day.

This saves you a lot of time and effort (plus food budget costs, too!) and will keep you from heeding the call of tempting fast food.

Why make bad choices on unhealthy fast food joints when you can just pop your head in the freezer and check for leftovers?

Besides, if you stick to the recipes and make your healthy meals with love, they're going to be so incredibly delicious that your whole family won't be able to resist leftovers the next day!

Entertainment Endeavors

When you want to get free entertainment, why not head out every so often?

You can check online guides about upcoming shows, concerts, outdoor craft shows, and fairs at each town you stay for a quick stopover.

Don't barricade yourself inside your RV all the time. Instead, make an effort to head out and skip the Netflix every once in a while.

Check out local museums and parks, flea markets, festivals, historical sites, as well as free entertainment at private campgrounds. This will help you save electricity and Internet bills—plus, you get to go out, stretch your legs, and soak in the healthy sun, too!

Conclusion

With all of these nifty tips and tricks and RV life hacks, you just can't go wrong!

Eating healthy meals has never been this easy and this affordable. All you really need is a little patience, some dedication, and a whole lot of love for food.

So go ahead and start heading out there as a healthier and happier RV-er today!

I sincerely hope this cookbook and healthy living guide has helped you in some way. It took me a while to gather and test the recipes, but it was worth every minute of my time.

If you would please leave a reivew of this book wherever you purchased it? I look forward to reading your feedback. I will certainly take your comments to heart and apply any suggestions to my future works.

Thank you so much for reading my book! I am humbled that you are interested in the same things that I love – travelling and staying healthy.